HACKER
PACKER

HACKER PACKER

poems

CASSIDY McFADZEAN

McClelland and Stewart

Library and Archives of Canada Cataloguing in Publication
available upon request

ISBN: 978-0-7710-5722-9
ebook ISBN: 978-0-7710-5723-6

Published simultaneously in the United States of America
by McClelland & Stewart, a division of Random House of Canada Limited,
a Penguin Random House Company

Library of Congress Control Number: 2014920838

Typeset in Janson by M&S, Toronto
Printed and bound in USA

McClelland & Stewart,
a division of Random House of Canada Limited,
a Penguin Random House Company
www.penguinrandomhouse.ca

1   2   3   4   5   19   18   17   16   15

 Penguin
Random
House

To my mother and my father
and to Nathan

CONTENTS

HACKER
PACKER

THE NIGHT BEFORE A RED-EYE FLIGHT

Even the bathroom vanity lights – mid-piss –
flicker at the drama of my leaving.

Newspaper headline says: *What to read
in 2015*. Don't read the text underneath.

I had a dream about a daddy-long-legs with no legs,
his whirling bulb still chasing after me.

I am disturbed by the things we do to get free.
Left my job at the library, shelving books

in slots already lodged with Doritos bags
and empty Coke cans. Sev is hood literacy.

There's a missing puzzle piece I wonder
if you've seen – the cartoon penis of a boy

overlaid with illustrated organs, then bones
then a layer of meat. Tell me if you find me

wandering the streets of Rome
wearing my clothes from two days before.

We return to places we've already been.
The path outside the city pulls us in.

Winter kept our footprints whole,
mud-covered fossils hidden under snow,

so walking on old steps weighs the negatives of who
we were against the imprints of what we've become.

This year, my body is locust-thwacked.
Their buzzing bodies struck my skin

and landed on tilled earth, whirling insects
like spinning tops animated from within.

There's an order to such tiny things.
Is our passage any less stupid or dizzy?

My fortune cookie promised
I'd meet *a stranger on an unpaved road*.

I found the blue jay with a cut wing in a tree.
His triangle gash shadow-painted branches.

Between two hills and the rusted tractors
abandoned in a straight line, we feel the weight of sky.

We're a tin can crushed by the rubber of your shoe.
We're the shell of a seed that splits in two.

We stand on red and yellow leaves,
the cloak of round petals peeled over ground

like mosaic tiles leading to the valley's portico.
In smooth pebbles at the river's bed

the stag emerges from still water,
his antlers, hands reaching from scattered stones.

I ride the chariot rail,   roam the billowroad
trammelled to soft skies,   sightseeing steering me
where flycatchers soar.   I flutter like a mastcloth,
my woundhue sign against   a seafoam of green.
I call on far countries,   comfortclothe swarms
of ritereaching hands,   heads twisted upward,
watching as I wander   the warped stony lane.
It takes me all day   to traverse my footpath
so I smile earwide   and wage timepassing tricks.
As faces follow,   I make figures swoon.
But I'm prickle-edged   and my icepiercing gaze
throws poison darts   deep into the eyes
of the bunches waiting   breathbated, limbquivering.
As I wave and go,   withdrawing by day
I leave their outfits   lifeless, deflated.
When I reappear   they'll praise me as a god.
Say what I'm called,   speak my name.

is rain-worn as the faces of horse and man
left on the Parthenon. The pediment recasts
its ghosts in overlapping sheets of plaster.
The supplement's presence whispers absence
as gypsum ambassadors wait for Athena's return.
Her peplos comes in thirty or it's free, we plead.
Museums are zoos where we see other countries'
breeds of griffins, nymphs, endangered stone beasts.

The gods lost in shipwrecks are half-eaten by sea
creatures. *In Ancient Greece, the substitution
of sculpted women for columns was not altogether rare,*
we read. There is a room with a row of caryatids,
some missing limbs, hair pressed against the ceiling.
Someone plays Haydn overhead.

The stars' swordmouths gleam above us,
speaking. Night says place the still-wet loess

horses inside the woodfired kiln. Wait, then see.
The figures hiss and steam over coals.

Heat separates the heads of horses from slender
bodies. We hear them pop. That's our world –

caught in the light, baked into shards. We gather
the windshaped sediment, mould clay into men,

lions, bears. Their limbs rain down upon us,
human arms and animal skulls falling like pellets.

Boom, gone. Yeah, we move on.

Under fluorescent museum light we examine
a vial of stardust, matter that formed us all.

Nothing's gone for good, nothing's ever new.
A factory worker fired my ceramic cruet.

I drop my crockery to hear it break on the floor.
Starlight touches my skin. I finger-sketch a horse

in the sand, and waves crash against the shore,
stealing mud. Water rushes in, now my horse

has bound. Pose for a bright flashing behind
my head: meteor shower, fireworks, bomb.

This time of year, Agamemnon's
tomb is swarming with Beliebers.
If I was your boyfriend, Clytemnestra . . .
What's the theme of this one, teacher?

We raised our iPhones in the dark
like gold-leaf masked talismans.
Our ringtones were a Greek chorus
calling from the hive to lion guards.

I'm a novel with the pages uncut.
Someone flipped me open and had enough.
Now reading me rips me in two.
What's a poem for? What's it to you?

Whoever said size don't matter lied.
The shaft of the cistern in the hillside
had me on my hands and knees.
I lapped up clay with my teeth.

We were catamarans in my last fantasy,
skipped in this world like a stone over sea.
You stole me away from the treasury.
Freedom, Siri, was a machine.

Window-seated, I watch men in yellow vests
lay metal ribbing across the garden.
Their hands are as intimate as the steel point
that mapped the faces of the bronze women

inside this room. The one closest to me crouches.
What am I but a woman on my knees, breasts bare?
This one's elbow juts out of stone clouds.
We glance into her marble pond and lose

track of which side reflects our world.
Everything hard becomes soft. See now,
Francesca's skin, polished milk, implores us
to reach out and touch the curves of her body.

We've nearly forgotten they're chiselled stone.
Ariadne's fingers figure larger than my own.
Her head leans on her hand, she smells the sawdust
we smell. Plaster hung in his workshop.

We know it well. The unfinished form, crude
in filtered light, shadows at her ribs. The devil's
hand cradles man – but the hand that sculpted my lips
freed me from my marble, then abandoned me.

My god didn't lose interest, he never had any.
His chisel marks – exposed or erased – ask
the stone to reach back out, an ambivalent,
sculpted shrug. A wax mask behind a sheet

of glass stares back at the sunken, sightless face.
You gave me speech. Talking to that quiet
part inside myself becomes me – yes –
and makes me not less alone, less lonely.

ON WEARING THE LEGGINGS OF EARTHLY DELIGHTS

Not are they born of the left-most panel – of fowl
        and fur emerging from a place of absence, from which
                we perceive a layer of brown earth. Nor from God blessing Eve,
        as Adam wipes the sleep from his drowsy eyes. Neither
has it come, this exquisite disguise, from a dragon

        tree breeding vines like fungi, a pink pyre half vegetative,
                half mechanical. Nearby, we find an albino giraffe grazing
        on flora as unicorns casually sip from a mirror-glinting pool,
a menagerie's weird vision that depicts a gale of birds
        swarming into archways worn into stone, as men carve

                huts into blue mountains, awarding them provisional homes.
        Nay, indeed, has my splendid armour been spawned
from the right-most panel – that grotesque chamber
        of globes, compasses, and knives turned against man
                and his fleshy ears grown gigantic. We find demons playing

        the instruments of our creation as toad kings suck
the marrow from our feet. But we'd wear not
        these chains tightening on our skulls with each
                tick of the metronome or strum of the golden lyre. We're
        trapped like swine as fur-covered beasts pitch tents

inside our guts' carved-out caverns. Their camps
        are lit by the lanterns of a city falling in the back
                regions of this burning hellscape laid out flat as a map
        missing its key. Like the lack of my idealized thigh
gap, it's the triptych's centre scene set behind

grisaille shutters opened like wings and transferred
        to a spandex canvas that clings to my gams. Figures devour
    larger-than-life strawberries on my ankles, sucking
pulp. Birds feed swollen lips on my calves
    as gleaming pearls burst from women's crevices

        resting in clams. Couples glide in buoyant spheres on a lagoon.
    While at my knees, I'm touched by eager arms clutching
for ripened fruit from the branches of my tree.
    My thighs host a battle scene: owls besiege their prey
        as nude knights ride in procession alongside swine and ass.

The pond dimples at my lower back, the floating globe
an alchemist's copper flask. I model a stream
    of life that gushes forth at my hips' curve, two creeks
        veering to a single lake as my body folds the triptych together,
    making it whole. Bearing this dazzling tapestry,

I wear his inventions – his beastly ardour,
    and fecund orchards, his eggs bursting with glaciers,
        jutting swords and fragile charms, a garden both swelling
    and crystalline – and he wears mine. Master of comely
visions, he gives me a leg up in this world.

One summer I   spoke Old English
in my professor's house   as he healed weeks
after a septuple bypass,   his stitches showing
out the top of his shirt.
                              We sat below a
picture of Danceland,   a prairie attraction,
its rainbow banner   a beacon above us.
My feet never brushed   the ballroom floor,
its famous horsehair   hidden under planks.

I didn't sing as Cædmon   charmed by a psalm
but stumbled through gruff   Germanic sounds.
My professor took breaks   propped up in a chair
while I watched his cat,   claws out, scratch
at the carpet and walls,
                              chasing a bell.
In that searing heat,   stayed to our places,
I sat and watched   workers rake,
men pull weeds,   women plant sod.

Slats of wood click together as I traverse
       the picture room. Slanted planks rise and fall
like waves crashing within a rocky cwm.

       Diagonal boards, shaded dark and light, form
an optical illusion, arrowheads that push
       us toward the walls. Faust juts out from

Rubens's orle. Romulus beckons Remus
       to drink of the she-wolf's bottle. As men step
forward, planks rise below. My glacier

       tilts underfoot. I wait for men to make
a movement I can follow. I wait for deep
       voices to pause so that I might speak.

The wood others have worn presses on
       my feet. Women in blazers and leather
boots assemble music stands, unfold metal

       skeletons, straighten flimsy spines, fan out
rib cages so sheets may be held in place.
       It is necessary to secure unfettered releases

of passion. The soldier tempers the Sabine.
       We sit in the Hall of Pietro da Cortona
to drink in his angle. The borrowed oil

       on canvas is armoured with Plexiglass, is
three-dimensional. Plastic shields it
       from our camera flash. The shutter clicks

like falling dominoes, led by pendulums
        of swaying cameras. Nikon lenses could be
millstones or medallions. Metronomes

        beat against pillowed breasts. Boots step
over clicking slats. Wooden panels are
        worn by our bodies' constant pulling apart

or coming together. We're a light-filled
        rift, one that's splitting from the next room on.
I feel your footsteps and follow along.

The peacock's tail display is amped-up paisley
on medieval tapestry. Flora and fauna intertwine
with palmettes against a botanical backdrop.
That it lacks a focal point upon which to rest our eyes
is not the crux of the fabric. We find a cheetah

climbing a vine while a griffin puzzles the blossoms
at his hind feet. Nearby, a monkey picks fruit
as a hound drools. Under lotus canopies, an antelope
peeks out. A phoenix hunts winged game.
Green obscures beasts dovetailing into the scene,

wool's warp that camouflages its position in the weft's
earthy seams. We fail to make out the leaves,
figures half disappearing into trees. Even the slant
of wing my eyes picked up lost its feathers
to viridescence, threads made solid in their spinning.

But what intrigues most hides in plain view:
the nearsighted botanist feels his way through
a catalogue of species. His footsteps wander
like cords winding around a coney's throat
and, tightening at our peering, they choke.

What you are now we used to be; what we are now you will be.

The friar's hologram greets us thusly. Says if our souls
are pure and good we will see a vision of immortality.
Think St. Pio of Pietrelcina. He bore stigmata for fifty
years. Here's an image of Jesus bleeding. Worse

than my monthlies? The red of his thorn crown disturbs
me. The friar was a good man. He walked with a wicker
basket collecting alms while sporting a metal vest
beneath his blouse. Teeth dug into his skin, rubbed

his flesh raw. Like a ribbon around his finger, pain
reminded him of sin. So he made penance by gathering
bits of bread and pails of milk. I'm hungry, can you fetch
me a snack? My whip chases the devil out of my fat

and strikes the switch that turns me on. We enter
the monks' undercroft and find six chambers candlelit.
Beside the mounds of holy dirt, I spy a human skull
with thigh bone wings, spiny light fixtures. Jaws locked

in intricate floral arrangements. Pistil, stamen,
mandible. Savour this. We enter the hall of pelvises,
the crypt of shin bones, skeletons with scythes crafted
artfully. The Princess of Barberini hangs from the ceiling.

We see couples drop to their knees. We are moved
along. In the Corridor of Exaltation, visitors lie
at the feet of friars half rotted away. Such displays
distract me from rear-wall detailing, a coat of arms

made of crossed arms. One clothed, one muscular.
How can I keep my memory of this moment clear?
Like cartloads of bodies pulled to the friary and air-
buried, time eats at our memories, no matter how dear.

Then the gift shop, and a woman I follow outside.
Her short black hair and Ray-Bans. Wedged heels,
tight grey jeans. I wanted to be her, in Rome,
and disappear down the street talking on an iPhone.

Cecilia's prayers trickled underground, carried
in a nearby stream. They were well-water hymns,
which tastes of calcite when drunken, shadows

flitting over the walls' shelves as the aqueduct's fish
hardened to their fossils. Cold trailed us in narrow
corridors as incense led. We were greeted by smoke

spectres of our families, the girl's body made still
below the water table. We knelt under trees, twisting
knobs smarting from absent branches. Three

lacerations on her effigy mark where her neck
wasn't slit clean off, dimpled like strawberries
with the seeds sucked out. Beheading something

made it a martyr, but the men took three slashes,
and left it to fortune. It was burial we pleaded for,
our fingertips needled with lamprey teeth,

sandpaper rows of indentations that clung to the fabric
of our robes. Our begging polished the pages of our
descendants' book of hours as nostrils deepened

on our necks and throats. The underearth smelled
of clay and water. The tunnels' dirt was pounded
together as volcanic rock hardened. We dug deeper,

and piled the bodies in mounds. As sockets hollowed
into our cheekbones, sun washed over the walls.
We ground pigment from ochre and stone, painted

frescoes of fish and bread loaves. Day brought
us to sing until the sky was sealed with brick.
Masonry brought darkness to our halls, as men

with pickaxes and satchels propped up fence posts
surrounding the crypts. When it rained, the bulwark
contained floating bodies. Around each corner

was another row of slots. We piled skeletons inside
the walls, like nectar hardening to its honeycomb.
Families shared tombs, bones rattling in cavities

like the plump ball bearings of a lotus seed pod.
Sprouting on our wrists, they were evil eyes.
We did not grasp the whole: that the child's milk

teeth must fall before her molars descend from her
skull, layered in her jaw, clustered, in waiting.
The ovals of the marbled cone snail were a warning

pasted on a mosaic shell. But Cecilia's breath never
quickened at venom: it was the holes in the walls
that pressed on her. The shadow growing at the end

of the corridor, under the earth where the air is thin
and cool. That blackness reached forward, from corners
where water seeped into layered rock. The weight

of our bodies pressed on her too. Our feet stepped
over bones and she looked up above the arcade
to the full moon and felt the suction of its craters.

My man, he keeps a birdhouse on
a pole, he does, a sparrow on a string.
We brandished wooden racquets, head
on handle, hit the birdie to its kin.

The plastic flies like feathers. Swivel
and it swoops. That's how birds soar,
singing. We swing our racquets, *whoosh* –
beaks gone noisy in their roosts.

Have birds in the morning always
been so chatty? Have pigeons ever cooed
this loud? The sun, it makes a racket
in its turning. It's shadowed in a cloud.

I have a sabo cat named Mishka, I do.
I hold a kitten on a rope. He wanders
rackets round the birdhouse, flounces.
His mews are carried in his throat.

A lighthouse draws us near it, little
snails in the sand. My muse runs
rackets in its beacon. Me? I'm coiled
in my turning, tentacle to lamp.

For stillness, drink white petals steeped
in hot water, chamomile flowers that unfurl
like ribbons skirting the bottom of a maypole.

Drink tightens my body also. Mud in my nostrils
sticks like manure, wet and heavy, as stir-crazy
robins eat of waterlogged seeds. Morsels

left too long under snowdrifts fatten with larvae.
Caught in a thaw, I'd almost dressed in white
and twirled with my twins, transforming into grace.

I'm becoming moist, the most fertile word my lips
know. The fauns who live in the woods next to
the graveyard stinking of its crematorium

taught me this. Their hooves sunk into earth as
pallid Zephyr grabbed my naked shoulders
and made me breathe roses. Now I scatter petals

when I exhale. Now I wear a floral-print gown
when I stand against the blossom wallpaper.
As the snow disappeared, dried leaves left over

from autumn flitted along the sidewalk's concrete.
I stepped over what I thought was a pair of leaves.
The shadow transformed into a sparrow's wings,

still hinged at the feathers, reaching its vanes
toward me. The wings were missing a skull,
and emptied of the bird's body and light bones,

an angel's set worn in a child's pageant. Wings
clipped to my hips, a prop of flight. Raised on
a rope, I'm silent as the seraph who shed them.

THE CHARIOTEER

His stony stare shines with opal and onyx.
How he's survived this long is beyond us.
Hiding for years in an earthquake's debris
still clutching the reins of his long-lost steed,

or pony – or whatever you'd ride.
There's a tunnel below the Temple of Apollo
we crawled inside, expecting to unearth
some prophesies. We breathed in the ethylene,

then left in a trance with dirt on our knees.
He escaped the lootings single-handedly.
I barely made it up Mount Parnassus
without stopping to pee next to some cows

and a freshwater spring. Going underground
was good for morale. All he knew was melted
down to bronze wafers. I'm waiting for a bus
in a fog, my pockets heavy with staters.

This long-necked   lackey lurks
at the forest's edge,   feints at trees' feet.
Statue-still,   he skulks in silence,
his arms primed   for approaching steps.
His master's rule   reaches far throughout
this creature's veins,   the core of his threads,
infecting his hand   with fated deeds.
His bloodlust beckons,   browbeats, pulls.
For when innocent   souls pass across
his road, this fiend   wraps his arms
firmly around   frightened throats,
tightens his clasp   as creatures shriek.
He steals his victims'   voices, reaps.
Who is this creature?   Say what I mean.

ON NAMING AND THE ORIGIN OF PITY

We called him George, an anachronism
in the grade eight classroom
where his old-fashioned name seemed out of place.
I knew a Clara and Araya too

– both killed by twenty-two, the obituaries said.
They were named for great-grandmothers they never met.
Linearity rejected them.
And just as the twins seemed never to speak a word
in all the hours of speech therapy we shared –
surrounded by phonemes and graphemes in English and Cree –
we all had our quirks.

George was burned all over
as far as any of us could tell. He was a tower above
the rest of us. He'd been held back.
His fingers clutched the strings of his hoodie hiding the edge
of his wax-tightened mask.
So when firefighters came to give a safety presentation,
it was George they had crawl on all fours

through the set-up of plastic tubes in the gymnasium,
and test the imaginary heat
of the wood of the fake door with the back of his hand.
We could almost see a younger George
starring in the locally produced vhs
they screened in the community room each year.
It would be a grainy George leaning into the metal garbage bin
to watch the red and orange flicker of flames

and being trapped within,
the boy's curiosity getting the best of him.

My father was a janitor, more or less,
at the Lawson pool a few blocks away.
Everyone came on Tuesday nights for Family Swim,
which was free, the pool sloshing with bodies.
Dad said he'd seen him there. Kept an eye out, I think.
It was hard not to: the melted skin

of George's face, its brush strokes of dried acrylic,
shined in the pool's cool light.
George was not so easily hidden from sight,
but it was a nice gesture for a kid my father barely knew.
He helped him get into his locker
when George had lost the key. And when he wrenched
open the metal, there were only some sneakers
and a balled-up T-shirt inside.
No towel or change of jeans. George on the third-storey tower

of the Lawson looked like any other kid –
the one who shot his friend
by accident and tried to burn the body
in the alley, for instance – his skin
just brown like the others instead of the pale pink
his scars usually looked.
He dashed and dove off the edge of the platform,
a blur through the air,
then disappeared under water.

SOLOIST

A piano is an animal's chest
propped open, ribs spread to better
hear the beating of its heart.

In childhood, we had to be told
when to clap, our bodies bussed
to the Centre of the Arts

after being coached on conduct.
We didn't waste time on what
we knew we wouldn't live to see

and good intentions came and went
like kids shipped from foster
homes to rez homes to Dojack

then back. It was another badge
of lack we wore, like speaking
words we'd only ever seen

on a page. The seams between
at-risk and asking-for-it
began to fray, some of us too old

to be subdued by music. Still,
we stayed to watch the fingers
of the pianist's right hand moving

like mechanisms becoming extensions
of the frame. The hammer pulled
back. His left stayed in his lap.

The strain pulled over our eyes.
Moved to our feet, we clapped
when we felt it. We did.

FLEDGING

In which home cannery inflicted botulism
via winging the diced tomato's acidity
and pH levels under pressure fluctuating.
We botched salsa for frugality and spousal

bonding. Outside, a raven heeded its mother's
tucked feet as it fell from its nest, made of bits
of twine and wwii headlines. We hauled a box
of clippings the old man's widow gave us,

yellowed from the rain and time. Lending
new meaning to memory foam, we filled
a piecemeal bed with matted horsehair, husks,
old rags, straw we'd scattered in the garden.

Bone meal and crushed feathers bettered
blooming for the growing of heirloom carrots.
Our cultivars were purple-bruised, needing
our hands' caress as pink whorls' folded lips,

a garter giving something old. Teeth pulled dirt
off my skin like moths eating lace in a hope chest's
closet resting place. Rust flies were drawn
to the vegetables so their larvae, when hatched,

burrowed into roots like lice inside the raven's
black lattice plume. A bird's-eye view caught
a shiny thing: paperclip, chess piece, pinhead
hidden from the rookery. Glinting, a gold ring

was rooted in the soil of an abandoned ski slope
beneath petrified triffids, rogue weasel pelts,
and snakeskins our hands shaped into a hydra.
We cultivated a bridleway used for bicycles

in summer days. The mountains – their twisting
roots – brought my man to me. Symptoms came
as double vision – age – but feverless, dug out
from soil, added to our menagerie's transection.

My eyes to its feathers darted from the window's
shutters. The ravens were thick-billed, sewn
with sawdust, mannequin's woodwool flown
from utility pole to ostensible Holarctic clade.

I'm made of pastel, that lightness mimicked
in a bundle of muted petals sewn from silk

and pasted together. Maidens bathe the pistils
in perfume, a mist that cloaks my nostrils

so I cannot think for sniffing. Dogtooth violet
hints at spring, its lilac fangs turned skyward,

a halo of grinning canines. Yesterday, my dentist's
arm rested on my rib cage between my breasts.

She told me not to swallow and to show her how
I floss. She held the vanity mirror like a lyre,

and I hid the blood beneath my tongue.
Like wreathes faded in the sun, I am lipstick

blotted on rose-tint Kleenex, a drought
that cracks my cupid's bow into tributaries,

pigment into rattling sticks. The laurel flowers
as a sea urchin. My fingers, leaves. It's

awful to suck the colour from all the things
you look at in this world and see.

We walk from our rented Ikea-furnished flat
in Viktoria-Luise Platz, past the KaDeWe
to the zoo's red elephant gate where Knut,
rejected by his mother, once lived. He died
alone behind an iron barricade as a hundred
looked on. Berlin's the first city we've been
where officers check our metro tickets.
They're dressed in plain clothes, and brandish
wireless scanners as they haul the woman –
still pleading her case – off at Hallesches Tor.
The Tiergarten's greener than chlorophyll
seems, even in its still somewhat frozen state.
The lake reflects a sparrow in a numbered
house, hanging by wire in the trees, roosting
out of harm's way. The playground appears
with a groan of a rusted roundabout, imprints
of children's spinning games. A swing set's
chains rattle as its slanted metal poles glimmer
iridescent like oil spilled in a pool. We take
a few pictures, find the empty sandlot aches
of the frigid March mornings back home. If
parks like these are rewards for history's
past feats, Zigaretten machines must be coping
strategies for future misdeeds. Farther along,
colonnades of trees frame bronze statues,
Prussian aristocrats' creations. They're greened
from oxidization, or envy of the Siegesallee's
leaf canopies. Twisting inventions are painted
with *soulsailor*: man attacks a lock-jawed fox
and spears its torso over his head like a banner,

tossing his own snarling dog to the ground in
a dynamic show of his whip's kiss. We marvel
at how a loose rope presents so much weight.
Beside this frozen scene, a living dog sniffs
a bush, tracking spoor. We pass a dead bull,
and a dead boar, and come to a narrow path
and a quiet square. We find a boy and a horse,
a bronze buffalo seated alone. When snow
covers this green corner, we return to the gold-lit
road. A tree's carved with lyrics to "Stand by Me."

Reports of Fern Andra's hijinks hit us
at Potsdamer Platz. We skimmed sensational
tabloids regaling daring shoots, aircraft accidents,
her marriage to a scar-pocked boxer. Her full

body paint caused quite an uproar, but Fern
was never happier than when perched on the harness
of her circus horse, or walking the tightrope,
swinging her weight across the striped tent

as she flexed her spine. Fern Andra, a spy?
Like raging wildfire the rumour has spread
that the actress was arrested in Berlin. Fern
falls out of fashion, and not soon after, boots

march through the Lustgarten for a larger screen.
A slender waist, her creamy skin. The album
of yellowed clippings could've been glued in place,
oh, say yesterday. Fern's celluloid smile fades.

In the next room, we pull open metal drawers
cool to the touch, heavy in their runners,
and watch a darker Olympia within.
A video on a loop starts to sing.

A face is shed on the highway. Fur is torn
away from muscle, a red mould in the crude

shape of the creature that lost it. Like a
cobbler's wooden last, its fur can be stretched

over bones, forming a sort of mask, filled
with sawdust and sewn. What of the other

woodland beasts? We pass a raccoon
in rigor mortis, nearly intact. The skunk

we know by smell, not stripe. We think
of stopping for the cat, but only to ensure

its stillness. Whatever rodent this used to be,
it's flattened now. Anything can be flayed.

From farther away, the tree appears to hold
a sparrow's nest among green walnuts.

The boughs hold tight to its trap. Cobwebs
glint halfway up a branch, thick with flies.

Every dense white cluster we see resting
in offshoots, flowerpots, or lattice is a skein.

I'm waiting on the porch, my place among
the spiders. Pull the string and let me in.

What maiden speaks   in murmurs, moans
as you hold her curved,   round waist, salivates
as you caress her neck,   clasping her buffed skin,
filling her drawn lips?   Leave her and she swells.
She trembles and sighs,   seething in slow suspense,
rumbling in fury and   raising hot breath.
She foams at the mouth,   frothy, back arched
before squealing out,   singing a sweet song,
heaving and gratified,   full-fed, released.
But study her shape   and she shies, ceases
her cooing and calms,   clearing like the sky
after a stormy fog,   wavesilent, still.
Who is this creature?   Call out her name.

THE UNICORN RECOGNIZES ITSELF IN THE MIRROR

The sunlight stabs its stabbing rays
right through the trees and iron frame

surrounding this whole estate. It's too
early to think, I think. It's that late.

History's so bright I gotta wear shades.
What's a tric trac anyway?

The exhibit's guard never explains,
flashes us a pamphlet riddled with dates.

No photos please, we can't Instagram
blurry shots of ancient erotic games.

I shiver to the frigidarium underneath,
and descend the stairs to a deeper gate.

This tapestry shows the unicorn came
and offered his horn to that slender dame.

He giveth her the sense of ecstasy.
She wielded it with mastery

and held up the mirror to give him sight.
The beast smiles back with shining light.

I was moved by this scene. I moved away
and touched the narwhal's horn on display.

How am I sentient in any case?
The clerk in the gift shop is so ornery.

Embroidered socks, embroidered cape.
The shape of his horn makes me horny.

CAMEO

The girls with daggers in their eyes
wove petals in our braids. We want
the curtain and the light box, the hood
behind the plate. We pull a shutter

on a string, stay frozen to our places.
Fishing for compliments, we catch
our own half-formed reflections.
We fill our pockets with river stones,

press baby's breath in book leaves:
ex libris of a girl brushing her hair
in negligee, broderie anglaise. We meet
a figure in a field and scatter hollyhock.

Our twins wear black capes against
our white lace. We bear crowns
of daisies hung in our travelling caravans,
cupboards rattling with saucepans.

We leap over a river's eddy to lie
in hillside grove. Eat of edible flowers,
dab on our necks crushed lilac perfume,
and finger a stone as pestle against

our deflated wombs. We grasp ornate
hand mirrors, engraved with filigree,
and the glass reflects our inner beauty:
hollowness we can't see inside.

Red lipstick we hid from our mothers,
beauty marks we blotted on our chins.
We sip chamomile tea, eat marzipan
shaped like things we don't eat, suck

the candies of Antoinette's orchard:
her preserves, her macaroons, vined
grapes in a glass behind the gold-plated
gates of Versailles. Beetles skitter

under rocks our brothers lift to show
us. Worms wriggle in the tunnels
our fathers mined. We lift pillows
on our beds and squirm at what we find.

is only visible after disembowelling it.
Its iridescent fins were aurora borealis
in the prairie night sky, its mouth

blue as a child's lollipop-stained tongue.
Wonder gripped us then, had us spear
the wandering thing from the basin's jetty,

its spots red as magma in our hands.
Knifing it gave us our prize: Smurf-
smooth flesh we didn't know existed

outside our imaginations. Its strawberry
blood rusted brown in our hands,
but its swim bladder was putty

we could almost lean in to mould.
We carved its flanks into folded lips,
strips that made us salivate when held

against the griddle's quiet sizzling.
Some insist no food is truly blue –
berries on the vine turn purple on the plate –

knowledge we now hold to be true.
The meat lost its pigment in the pan,
turned off-white as its widened eyes.

The tree bough was shed of its casings,
surface almond-blanched in paleness
I didn't see until spring when rain prompted
me to look above. My fingers kneaded
a fallen branch, smoothed bark from stem.
The curled lichen, eating at pith, made
dancing branches seem closer to those
Van Gogh painted on blue for his nephew
and namesake. Blossoms sing of new life
even in their writhing, but clearing flecks
of old bark made the plant seem too clean.
Had its albino layer, seemingly whittled,
been beaver-gnawed, we might have forgiven
its pristine appearance, thinking it a tic
of nature, inexplicable as fruit encasing hull,
green and deceiving. We called it a drupe,
and shucked its skin from body after boiling,
seed squeezed between fingers. Coat loosened,
it revealed an embryo as white as blossoms,
marzipan centre seized. Interlocking rivulets
of moss spanned the height of the tree, taller
than I am. Would the hollowed trunk fit
me inside it, if we shrink some in death,
moisture tightening our features? It might
be felled like the oak on the corner lot
that took out our porch window one storm.
A sucker grows from its stump, and I passed
it and the duplex across the street, where cops
routinely knocked on the basement doors.
I thought the tenants scattered plastic grass

on the real grass for Easter, indifferent
to the rabbits that might ingest the strands
and choke. I held this belief until I came
closer to see blue flowers covering the lawn
like a blanket, petals cast over hard eggs
of purple and green, halves crushed as squirrel
chased squirrel, birds chirped a cappella.
Spring's thrown voices had me duped.

I want to be a cover girl on The Bay's glossy flyer,
draped in a Hudson's Bay blanket, four stripes.

My casket's red on white. My wool's laced with virus.
Beaver pelt, jockey hat. I'm the hunter, you're the muskrat.

Forget the fur trade, let's role-play. I ambush
your lowly fortress. I commandeer this loaded musket.

You march the meandering path of Lieutenant Edgar Dewdney,
retreat to the pawnshops and Kokum's Bannock Shack.

Broken windows, shattered glass. All the city's streetlights
black out when I pass. All this city's roads split

from Dewdney Ave. I spot the old Government House
on Google Street View. Drag a cursor to the park

where Louis Riel hanged. Stand beside the flagpole,
can't make out the plaque. My flag flies at half-mast.

My leaf's white on red: that's a picture of the future.
Zoom into a pixelated cloud shaped like a boot print.

ARRHYTHMIA

Some terror inside me,
a clump of cells in my abdomen,

is sprouting straw-stiff hair.
I pluck the wax-coated strands

from my navel, each blade reeking
of vinegar and honey.

My stomach rattles with cut teeth.
Biting is how my teratoma

talks to me. It nags,
my valve's galloping rhythm skipping

between first and second sound
as tremors move in me like jockeys.

Bolting from the starting gate,
that was my rider flung

from his harness to the cuppy track
and I am the colt who moves

with ambling gait. My hooves deny
a canter's three beats, which are innate,

for those tongues hounds speak. I want
flames to mount and break me

when I still cannot talk for stuttering
which is always. Still,

I am woken in the night by vapour
escaping from glass chambers,

the vase's long snout breathing its vessels
of flowers released in moon hours.

It eases out from within, and squeals.
I stuff cotton in my ears, sublimation

that amplifies my breath
and my blood flow, louder in respite.

Its cawing unravels me,
a thread I draw out from my gut,

the cupped palms of cotton Ewen plucked
from an Alabama field

while I waited behind the gate.
He brought me four bolls like a bouquet,

capsule's burrs pricking my skin
like weevils. I had to get out and see

it wasn't just the props of movies:
rows upon rows of white,

and me feeling a beak in my belly
winding the whiteness into strings.

He sewed into me a clove.

HABITS

Her off-white veil came in the mail.
Held in packing nuts, its lace was imitation silk.
The mantilla's crocheted petals reeked of mothballs,
of wineglasses kept in the china cabinet

and paraded out annually on New Year's Eve
when children clinked ginger ale rims together.
The steam released from a hot shower
didn't cure its creases, but a hot tub baptism

in an inner-city gymnasium never hurt.
Children dove in. Pastor Tim clasped his Good Book
as he turned on the bubbles of his holy jet stream.
Once I got underneath, I never felt so clean.

Her veil unravelled like a jellyfish,
that first new breath its sting.

We saunter over the city's cobblestones
made rain-wet and smooth as Plasticine,

Via Argentina nearly malleable on my feet.
Our mud prints lounge in the doorway

of the Gammarelli where the next pope's
clothes undergo final fittings before

a smoke cloud appears in the chimney.
The bus sighs to its stop in Trastevere,

and takes us to Termini, where arrivals
slash departures domino into place.

Shutters turn like blades of grass
as Jupiter shushes the lawn to its side.

Nokia's default ringtone sounds
and an older woman in Nikes, a felt

floral hat, leopard-print blazer, searches
her purse. A man nearby answers the call.

As we ride past roofs of buildings planted
with TV antennae, clotheslines sway

with windswept wheat. Steel offshoots
bring satellite radio whispering the news.

BENEATH A GOLDEN ALTAR

This bishop's regal   resting place
is in a glass enclosure,   a gleaming cage
where his body has long   lain on display,
bones glossy   and grit with glaze,
beneath a golden altar   and angel's gaze.
Dressed in vestments,   he's doomed and fated
to tarry, ever flanked   by twin figures
on either side,   saints treasured,
and clothed in white   with crowns of gold,
palm leaves saved   for centuries.
In this crypt beneath   the basilica, the skeleton
sleeps in slippers,   snoozing in a mitre,
his eternal slumber,   his smiling teeth
like Sleeping Beauty   if the sultan never came,
like Briar Rose   if reaping was her game.
A ghost in a window,   a waking dream.
Who is this creature?   Say what I mean.

A raven hanging on the eaves beaked me,
his squawk heckling me so, I heard nearby
oscine like throat songs: the world's made

guttural. My lips parted to sky, reading
my hunger for thirst. I'm no augury,
but drank birdsongs inside me, fattened

with tweets, and cracked wise. On my way
outside, a plague doctor with his pomander,
long hooked beak, and spectacles met me

at the door. He who taps his cane on my
welcome mat surely wants for more.
We walked on brick as a dead crow landed

on the lawn. Its face was turned away, feathers'
vanes unravelling their threads. The quills'
hollow shafts exposed like stage props,

barbs frayed to their hooks. Nothing
could be undone. Its wings folded over,
a dummy of the bird perched on the duplex.

Immense and clumsy, its glossy weight
was lessened in death. Back alley power
lines clung to its wings like cobwebs.

DISCOVERY

We walked through the gallery made up
like a movie set. Its objects were arranged
just so, in rooms scored into cross-sections.
We could peer in from behind a velvet
rope or spend a little time inside, imagining

ourselves part of some other life. The plush
dolls and plastic Game Boys were artifacts
we discovered from behind glass.
Reading placards of the displayed gadgets,
we moved through decades, hurried into

the kickshaw shops, magic lanterns propped up,
and stopped to capture a photograph outside
the herbal apothecary. By the time we reached
the saloon, the night guards were already
on patrol. They blocked off narrow hallways

leading to exhibits we hadn't yet visited,
turned down the lights, paused the flit
of the Chaplin film on repeat. We had no
time to examine each of the antique devices
(the city police lantern, circa 1890), turn

the unfamiliar metal in our hands or try
to understand how the older generations
might have survived cold nights. Elsewhere,
your dearest friend lulled in a hospital bed,
lapsed in old age that couldn't be fixed.

She told us of pasts when we asked, but I still
couldn't grasp it. My last pic's a blurred ship,
the word *Discovery* painted on it. The cabin
holds a writing desk and chair, and a globe
of the earth, the seas we might still roam.

PAN AND THE SHEPHERDS

All my thoughts are about my dick.
What else? I stand in the thick of it.
The devil hangs between my thighs.
His reddened face is circumscribed.

I wouldn't call myself an opportunist.
I saw an opening so I took it.
I needed closure so I filled it. I'm fixed
to a formula – I go with what sticks.

My cock's head feathers are *au courant*.
He reaches out from behind the blinds,
and crows in the morning, raising his neck.
He spits up like a babe held to my breast.

I sate my babe's tender mewling while
the devil swells inside my abdomen.
His organ plays me down to hell.
Music brings me to heaven, and back again.

My pantry's onions softened
in burlap as last autumn's potatoes
wrinkled with mould, starch turning
to rubber. Their eyes sprouted eyes,

affording discerning devourers
a second sight. On the next shelf,
putty adhered itself to the bottom
of the stoneware crock. Prodding

our specimen named it: decades
old and yet unspoiled, honey
will sweeten the journey ahead.
We uncorked jars of dried fruit –

slabs of peaches petrified to papyrus
sheets. Our tongues read the map
of our downward path. The trowel
in our hands started digging it.

GNOMIC

You moved inside me, gnome,
as if I were an oak you chiselled out.
And you built a spiral staircase
with the rings you carved out,
polishing my handrail to a smooth
finish you adorned in arabesque,
incising acanthus in swirling
helixes. As though I'd swallowed
a whorl, your fingers strummed
my balusters as your boot soles
sprinted up and down my steps.
Nails you tapped into my chest
were a faint pinch, but it was not
until you hung portraits of kinsfolk
in blue tunics and red pointed caps,
fawns painted in miniatures
of your former haunts – forests
and pathways now grown over –
that I found your weight too vast.
You swayed inside me like
a compass trembling on a raft.

This is not an exit, reads the sign.
And it's not the way we got inside.
We retrace our footsteps as incense
surrounds us like a winking oculus.

We extend a maple branch, its leaves
dry into hands clasping our shadows: five curled
fingernails scuttle along the marble portico.
Blood's smeared on the seat of Peter's Dome,

a grisly scene from Bernini's gilded throne.
Holy velvet curtains are manned by Swiss guards.
There's a place for prayer and sacraments.
No point when you can't Instagram it.

Recall the solo euro to light up Moses.
He grasps his stone slabs as the story goes.
Our coin clinked inside the tin device.
There's Moses, come to life.

There's Peter's tomb inside the crypt.
The way inside is through the vents.
Sneakers pass above our heads.
Sing softly if you must sing to the dead.

Camera flashes illuminate relics.
Craning necks are something phallic.
Our foggy lenses read the room.
The way outside is through the tomb.

WHALE WATCHING

We had no blubber to shield us from the ache of air,
only a thin orange toque, a beacon
to the male sea lion, fat and naked,
resting on a boulder throne.
He was bound by crew and concubine,
moaned as our boat passed his wharf,
our cameras mounted to masthead,
shutters winking to grasp him.

Later, I met his brother on painted Styrofoam,
next to the lifelike woolly mammoth.
We never spotted any killer whales, but it's
probably for the best. What creatures swim
beneath our inflatable boats skim
over shells. We devour the rest.

I wanted to go where the mountain goat,
cloven hoof balanced over precarious
ledges, roams. So we packed a satchel,
and drove prairie back roads, foraging
for the tallest slope, or loftiest knoll.

We scoured atlases with a fine-toothed
comb, guided by aerial views clasped
like totems. Like all good legends,
the key revealed the abject lack of what
we'd come to see: topography green

to the neatline. We were resigned to rifle
for what we could not find. It was as if
within every chasm and crevasse stood
an oversight. Not a plateau, but a fracture
in the plate under our feet cracking like

a porthole. But the butte was bluffing
its lookout, its shale a slap in the cliff
face to summit seekers. Though Cypress
Hills offered a wrinkle of ridge upon
which I grasped your fingers, a handhold

to pass over crag, the mudslide stumped
us both. Even when we scaled the chain-
linked fence of St. Victor's petroglyphs,
and clambered up to touch its ancient
inscriptions with naked skin, hugging

the stone like a twin, glancing down
the thirty-foot drop-off still didn't startle us.
Were we overlooking the at-hand peak
for a yet unmet precipice, our harnesses
tied to the treeline? We drove from day

to night to Castle Rock, our stored image
of a citadel a last scarp. The keep jutted
out of cattle farms surrounding it, as birds
on all sides flew too close to the wire. Like
a fog brimming at the apex, they whirled,

and as we turned a winding road, a sparrow
hardened to our grill, wings stilled but intact.
We glanced down the fortress's earned view,
pinnacle's vision made slight by the crest
of the no sure footing we found we stood on.

It was a full moon, autumnal, when we waded the bayou,
dodging gators under an orange hue. We carved
cacti with the same three letters engraved
on Marie Laveau's tomb, and circled them
in crayon once the wish came true. Holding
to grace, we emerged in Hickory Hill's graveyard
of non-perpetual care, where children are buried
beneath pewter statues of laced-up roller skates
and skipping ropes. We let our legs guide us,
pressing gently to the arrow of our Ouija board.
Hands placed parallel on the grocery cart's
steering rod, our touch led us down aisles
for melons, squash, and other gourds. We feasted,
then woke up with red eyes, brackish creeks.

BORN OF A WOLF

Like a shallow pond   you peer within
and find a strange   reflection staring,
versions of myself   veer to the surface.
My habit is peculiar.   You've probably heard
of such troubadours: the travelling minstrel
whose timbres resound   in soothing trills.
A booster of morale,   his melodies swaddle
the peasants en masse,   moved to a stupor.
But the barge I rode   in on bore me to rail,
not to pacify swarms   or subdue with charms.
I was born of a wolf,   my ballads a whorl
which brings no comfort   but those held in cleaving.
To swing my blade,   singing on whetstone,
at man's deepest pain   or dullest cramp,
and cut a keyhole   to his cloisters is my claim.
The song I unlocked   will linger inside you:
it's a tag you'll find   you can't unfasten
and must wear stamped   on your skin instead.
You who invite me inside   your esteemed estates
to stand as a humble   servant in your home
will insist on ordaining me   your putative hermit.
Once was named *scop*,   once was named *skald*,
once scoffed in saga   and scolded in song –
I am a shaper of worlds.   What am I called?

I

I stepped beneath horned gargoyles on lookout:
twisted figures with skin folded over, half-shadowed
faces with jaws hanging open. Stone formed

an archway to step through. It was a fairy circle's
protection, a winding pathway that signalled asylum.
I met my guide on the cobblestone walk, stretching

a furlong, and passed below iron gates, shaved of rust
and restored. We held to the hanging garden, wielded
a green wall and its honeysuckles as spike mosses

crawled up brickwork. We gripped trumpet vine,
its fortune's spindle, winter's creeper, ivy bittersweet
as coral bells, the common hop we clung to.

II

We climbed erstwhile wonders of the ancient world,
now lost to lesser birds of paradise. Heaven-descended,
they hovered in our atmosphere drinking sky dew –

wingless birds – and made weightless flight. They flew
down chimneys along an uphill road below the chemist's
grave. At the side of the church, the ragged cliff face

overhung the bread shovel and his stove's specious fire.
He transformed flour into *eau de vie*. Isn't that enough
proof if it's proof you need? Atoms of this world beat

against me. That a forget-me-not's stem both resembles
a scorpion's tail and treats its venom is a rhyming that
resounds in all earthly things. We sought purification

in distillation, things reduced to mercurial substances;
cooked, digested, and fixed, the bodily, into incombustible
sulphur; fermented and divided into a perfect tincture.

Her fuchsia breast, her canary plume, I caught the majesty
of her song, captured in a cage in the corner of his room.
He'd hanged it from the wall, and nailed her bones in place.

III

Hedge woundwort ground into paste formed a panacea
for cuts, leaves serrated as wolves' teeth. That ancients
used colanders makes life seem commonplace. They beat

flour with yeast, smoothed dough into intaglio scratches,
metal worn and placed upon the carving plate. The kitchen's
pastry mould took the shape of a rabbit. Fill it with dough

and watch it rise. Splayed, its eyes were closed slits.
We bound its feet and paws, measured its spine with layered
stones. Provenance of Pompeii's ashes, of figures curled

in fear, we baked. We brought rabbits to the curios table
and exposed them to flames. A transformation of knives
against bread. You take the feet, I'll eat its coney face.

CUTTLEFISH

What's stranger in this world
than surfaces we've only skimmed,
or slipped over as the shoreline,
hardening to ice? The cuttlefish

camouflages itself in clear
water over white sand and waits.
Unless we make out the boundaries
between substance and its frame,

we might grasp it like water in our hands.
We wade deeper, the fish's skin
gashed with sharp rocks, kelp-veined,
overlaid with forests of algae.

Seaweed on arches flips our footing
to sand shards we magnify as castles
and rods. Green sceptres and whorled
shells of broken pottery propels us

toward it, something hardening
inside each of us. A bone's caught
in the mesh netting's float line,
an ink blot loosening, and hangs.

The dried leaf was a mouse, brown stem its tail.
Stepped over crushed eggshell,
membrane that holds its pieces together.
Translucent film was not pierced by heel or beak.
It was foolscap we shined with lead,
graphite imprints polishing our hands.
We see inside a window, the lotion by the bed.
See past the slit in the drapes
to the lace in the glass of the doorway.
A shadow of a square sign is carved into a
tree trunk at night. A saw has seen some stuff,
often the inside of my chest, as when I've swallowed its teeth.
Sing a lullaby for its cleaving,
those of us sensitive to that invisible realm.
Perceived in moonlight, it becomes heavier.
It hangs. I look into the darkness
and darkness is all I see. I sidestep to unlit streets,
my body indistinguishable from a tree.
Squirrels dart from bush to truck, clutching walnuts.
Our walking disperses the bird flock resting in grass.
Our presence disrupts the eating of worms.
No birdsong beneath the surface, only swallowing.
No chew, only gullet.
We cunning foxes smell of pine,
of needles crushed beneath our paws.
The sandpaper pads of our feet patter along the dusty pathway,
soft as silk or nearly so.
Charred walnuts are cracked open,
their shells left at my burrow's stoop.
In childhood, I left a Styrofoam cup

on the windowsill to catch the sunlight.
From soil dark with water sprouted a stem from the bean.
We watched it curl as it reached from the rim,
roots skirting its abdomen,
flitting green until we tore it.

I've no salve against a sudden stitch,
saxifrage being out of season,
and waybroad wilting at the roadside,
my storerooms likewise bare.
So I clasped at my twinge uselessly,
and held to that place of unsteadied seizing
as a trooping procession passed under a linden.
I was elf-shot, an arrow lodged
in my rib cage like a pebble
in tubers, which tighten as they burrow
deeper into dirt. Turning on itself,
my dart rooted itself inside me.
Out little spear, if herein it be!
But if it were God's shot, who would help me?
A whippoorwill isn't seen with eyes,
rather, hearkened back to in the night
by its call. This nightjar
makes its nest in the ground
and in fallen leaves mottled as its breast –
nettles and feverfew,
a cure for certain maladies of the body:
those the mender cannot easily see in you.
But song only heals if accompanied
by deeds. And so gestures, if wedded
to rhyme. Elseways, to grip this
embedded barb? Mere warbles and pantomime.
Out, little spear, not in! If I were shot
in the body, or shot in the skin,
or shot in the bone, or shot in the blood,
or shot in the limb, I would inscribe

Christ's mark upon me –
and so be cured, my spine
from paresis, and so ride.

You ever eat a pear
while walking down the street

and all that pear juice
is pouring down your cheeks?

Sweet juice drips down chins.
You can't help but grin,

pear juice being drawn to skin.
Spring is the time to begin again.

That swan raised its white neck
and attacked me at the Temple of Love.

I fled the park's wooden benches
and sat against its marble columns.

More and more each day,
I resemble Marie Antoinette,

slender chin cut from slender neck.

Most of this is coffee and metaphors,
and mornings waking up in the dark.
When lightning hit the gable,
it shook our bed, made the radio
short out, left our fingers tingling.
And when I asked you to touch my skin
I almost believed I'd see sparks,
almost thought we'd both be singed.

But others felt it too, the dark cloud
above our houses. We were not alone
in thinking light had left its traces
of ozone where we slept under sheets.
That surge of blue light engulfed
us like a wick, left us wanting.

Of the earth layered beneath
the surfaces of our visible world –
dirt under grass, river, concrete;
the places I step in the morning
out of bed, my skin imprinted
with the blankets of my sleeping.
Of a layer of blackened soil
wet and smelling of groundwater;
of silt, crawling with worms
and legs of teeming centipedes . . .
All things grow from darkness.
Roots curl, cutting tunnels under
stones. Grass strands dipped
in mud like inkwells become
fountain pens that sketch cross-
sections of our bodies. They turn
us into trees with the boughs

lopped off, theirs an act
of making. I slept beneath the earth,
in blackness without a night lamp.
My other self being away for a week,
I was without window or starlight.
And upon hearing of Maria's
departure from the physical world,
couldn't help myself from imagining
an intruder entering my room: he
stronger than I am and what recourse
I would have taken from me.
Or the ruin of my own volition,

passed out, face up in vomit.
I opted to sleep on my stomach,
downed a glass of water, phantom-
smelled my own decay, mused on
who would find the body and when,

pray. Of Maria's failed liver
at twenty-four, the same age I am
now. I anticipate a whiplash feeling,
nearly familiar as the others who've
already departed this solid place –
my friends and former bullies –
when I pass her on my next birthday,
and each after and each passing day,
how she will be remembered.
My mother reminds me that not long
ago Maria called the house, and
asked for me. But I was at school
or elsewhere, as I am now. Away.
Still, she promised to come visit
if she ever returned from Calgary . . .

I watched a car going the wrong
way down a one-way. The driver
was smiling, his passengers
unconcerned by his reckless shortcut.
The bleating horn of the oncoming
car was a trumpet call to the man
carrying a child down Market Street.
That's how Maria came to me:
her sister knocked up and kicked
out of Sacred Heart at thirteen.
We delighted in controversy,

the unfairness of it –
of our feminine possibilities.
We wanted to write and sing.
We wanted to move our bodies
in rhythm with the music we heard,
not made smaller by the weight
of the sky bearing on our ribs,

buried under buildings, pushed
into earth. And we sang
in my grandmother's basement,
where spiders tunnelled into dirt,
and dropped above our heads
like messages lowered on a string,
their webs spun taciturn. Maria
danced beside me in the cellar,
cool under the topsoil, windows
cutting off roots from sky. We ate
cucumber-and-chip sandwiches.
We watched MuchMusic videos:
the sway of women's bodies, of
Aaliyah, of Lisa Left Eye. Traded
my grandma's Valentine's Day
chocolate for Maria's blue lollipop,

preferring the sucker to the heart shape.
Music came from us on borrowed instruments.
She was on saxophone. I was on flute.
We played tentative notes, our
melodies on loan, woodwinds
in need of tune-ups, her reeds
squeaking. I was quick to untwist
feet from my body, undo body

from neck. I laid my silver metal
lips to rest and closed the hinges
of my case. But Maria polished
her brass like a child with a cloth,
pressing the fabric against her body
as though her fingers' touch alone
could erase the scratches to shine
the discarded instrument –
as if song would pour out from
the self-made mirror in her hands.

There is something twisting beneath us.
Even migrating geese can feel it.
It sprouts from bulbs of trees' hacked-
off branches, their phantom limbs.

Spring, this year, will bring
change – or more of the same.
It only depends on your state of mind,
your movement in the lull of days.

Everything depends on me and you.
The old wheelbarrow's been painted blue.
We reach out of earth's soil mounds,
feel the sky looming over our hands.

We are the roots writhing beneath
wood-block prints of the almond tree.
You see the blossom covered in dust?
That pink thing – untwisting – was us.

The answers to the riddles on pages 4, 24, 36, 49, and 61 are: sun, snare, kettle, body of Saint Ambrose, and poet.

"Thermal Shock, Dolní Věstonice" takes a line from a Selena Gomez song.

"You Be the Skipper, I'll Be the Sea" takes a line from a Justin Bieber song.

"The Ship Shall Be Nailed, the Shield Bound" takes its title from an Old English gnomic verse, and mentions David Thauberger's silk-screen of Danceland in Watrous, SK.

"As She Talks, Her Lips Breathe Spring Roses" takes its title from the Boyle/Woodward translation of Ovid's *Fasti* and was written with Botticelli's *Primavera* in mind.

"The Charioteer" mentions staters, or ancient Greek coins.

"Fledging" mentions the Holarctic clade, a taxonomical term for the common raven.

"Born of Lycia, Light of the Sun" and "Born of a Wolf" are epithets referring to Apollo.

"The Unicorn Recognizes Itself in the Mirror" refers to the Cluny unicorn tapestries.

"Remedy" takes lines from the Old English charm *Wið færstice*.

"To Bear All Toil and Wake the Clear Nights Through" takes its title from William Ellery Leonard's translation of Lucretius.

"Boomwortels and Other Roots" refers to Van Gogh's *Tree Roots and Trunks* and *Almond Blossoms*.

ACKNOWLEDGEMENTS

Some of these poems previously appeared in *Arc*, *Carousel*, *Grain*, *The Fiddlehead*, *Fjords Review* Online, *The Malahat Review*, *The Nashwaak Review*, and *The New Wascana Anthology*. I am grateful to the editors of each. Thanks as well to *The Walrus* Poetry Prize and the CBC Literary Prizes for featuring my work.

Some of these poems were written with the support of a Saskatchewan Arts Board grant, for which I am grateful.

I am indebted to my classmates and instructors at the Sage Hill Writing Experience, the University of Regina, and the Iowa Writers' Workshop, environments where I was surrounded with poetry and conversation.

Thank you to Medrie Purdham, Michael Trussler, Jeanne Shami, John Lent, Jeramy Dodds, Ken Babstock, and Mark Levine for introducing to me the music and magic of poetry. This book would not exist without your guidance.

I am hugely grateful to Kevin Connolly for your keen eye in editing this collection, and to Anita Chong, Ellen Seligman, and everyone at M&S for making this book a real thing.

Thank you to the Mader family, and to Risa Naytowhow, Coby Stephenson, and Kelly-Anne Riess for your beautiful friendships.

Thank you to my parents, Catherine and Thomas McFadzean, for ceaselessly believing in me. Thank you to my brothers, Dakota, Jonah, and Credence, for inspiring me with your ridiculous imaginations.

All my love to Nathan Mader for your clear-sighted reading of my work, constant encouragement, and exploring with me this strange world.

A NOTE ON THE TYPE

Hacker Packer has been set in Janson, a misnamed typeface designed in or about 1690 by Nicholas Kis, a Hungarian in Amsterdam. In 1919 the original matrices became the property of the Stempel Foundry in Frankfurt, Germany. Janson is an old-style book face of excellent clarity and sharpness, featuring concave and splayed serifs, and a marked contrast between thick and thin strokes.